Canadian National Railway

Steve Goldsworthy

Weigl

Published by Weigl Educational Publishers Limited
6325 10th Street SE
Calgary, Alberta T2H 2Z9
Website: www.weigl.ca

Library and Archives Canada Cataloguing in Publication Data

Goldsworthy, Steve
        Canadian National Railway / Steve Goldsworthy.
(Canadian business)
Includes index.
ISBN 978-1-77071-533-2 (bound).--ISBN 978-1-77071-534-9 (pbk.)

        1. Canadian National--History--Juvenile literature. I. Title.
II. Series: Canadian business (Calgary, Alta.)

HE2810.C14G65 2013   j385.06'571   C2012-907899-9

Printed in the United States of America in North Mankato, Minnesota
1 2 3 4 5 6 7 8 9 0 17 16 15 14 13

072013
WEP130613

Senior Editor: Heather Kissock
Art Director: Terry Paulhus

Weigl acknowledges Getty Images, Alamy, Newscom, CP Images, and CN as the primary image suppliers for this title.

Every reasonable effort has been made to trace ownership and to obtain permission to reprint copyright material. The publishers would be pleased to have any errors or omissions brought to their attention so that they may be corrected in subsequent printings.

We acknowledge the financial support of the Government of Canada through the Canada Book Fund for our publishing activities.

Contents

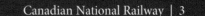

Introduction

For more than 90 years, the Canadian National Railway Company (CN) has kept both passengers and goods moving across Canada. With ports on both the west and east coasts, CN helps businesses import and export goods worldwide. CN also extends its reach outside of Canada, transporting goods into the deep south of the United States.

Operating since 1919, the Canadian National Railway Company is one of the oldest, most firmly established businesses in the country. The company began as a government-controlled **crown corporation** that often struggled financially. Today, it is a thriving multinational corporation with more than $9 billion in annual **revenues**.

CN's main line runs through the southern part of Canada, winding through the Rocky Mountains on its way to and from the west coast.

From Coast to Coast

CN operates more than 34,000 kilometres of track in Canada, making it the largest rail network in the country. It is North America's only **transcontinental** rail network. CN's railroads span the nation, from the coast of British Columbia to the coast of Nova Scotia. Tracks run from the shores of Great Slave Lake in Canada's Northwest Territories, to the Gulf of Mexico in the southern U.S. state of Louisiana.

> "To meet our customers' transportation and distribution needs by being the best at moving their goods on time, safely and damage-free."
>
> —*Canadian National Mission Statement 2013*

Keeping Industry Moving

The Canadian National Railway Company carries goods for various industries, from automotives and retail, to housing and energy. At any time, a CN train can be transporting natural resources, such as petroleum, metals and minerals, forest products, grain, and coal. Chemicals and fertilizers are also shipped from place to place on CN rail lines. The company specializes in **intermodal** service, in which goods are packed into large containers for shipment. The containers can be transferred from trains to trucks and ships without repackaging. Intermodal service has allowed CN to become one of the leading transportation providers in North America.

Large cranes load containers onto trains for transport to locations throughout North America.

COMPANY SNAPSHOT

Revenues (2012)

$9.9 Billion

Employee Total as of 2012

23,430

Rail Freight Distribution 2012

- Automotive 6%
- Petroleum and Chemicals 18.3%
- Intermodal 22.3%
- Metals and Minerals 12.7%
- Forest Products 14.9%
- Grain and Fertilizers 17.8%
- Coal 8%

Taking Stock

Founding Date
June 6, 1919

Became Public
November 17, 1995

Stock Symbol
tsx: CNR
nasdaq: CNI

Creating the CNR

In the late 1800s, Canada was a rapidly growing country. Much of this expansion was westward, with people moving to the Prairies and British Columbia in search of farmland and a new life. Many people arrived in the west via train.

The "last spike" had been driven into the Canadian Pacific Railway (CPR) in 1885, creating Canada's first transcontinental railroad. The CPR was crucial to the growth of the country of Canada. The railroad allowed the transport of new Canadians across the country. It also allowed industry to expand, building new homes and factories as well as moving resources and goods.

Canadian Pacific Railway director Donald Alexander Smith drove in the "last spike" at Craigellachie, British Columbia, at 9:22 am on November 7, 1885.

Over time, other companies began to see the value of having a strong railway system in the country. These companies began building railroads of their own to transport people and goods. By the turn of the 20th century, several railway companies operated along the thousands of kilometres of track throughout the country. As with the CPR, these railways did much to encourage settlement. Canada grew as the railroads went farther into frontier lands.

Federal Control

Many of these railways were built using loans from British banks. The companies were still relying on bank support when World War I broke out in 1914. The war brought several challenges to the railway companies. Fewer people were moving to Canada, and fewer goods were shipped during the war years. This meant less income for the railways. As well, the British banks that had been supporting the railways were now focussed on helping their own country survive the war. Many of the railways experienced serious financial hardship.

In order to keep Canada's trains on their tracks, the federal government decided to take action. In 1918, it assumed control of the near bankrupt Canadian Northern Railway. It also took ownership of a series of smaller railways, such as the National Transcontinental Railway and the Intercolonial Railway.

Canadian National Railway Company

The government began the process of amalgamating these railways as a crown corporation. On June 6, 1919, the new corporation was established as the Canadian National Railway Company. Over the next several years, CN assumed control of other railway companies. By 1923, Canadian National ran on more than 35,000 kilometres of track, making it the country's most extensive railway system.

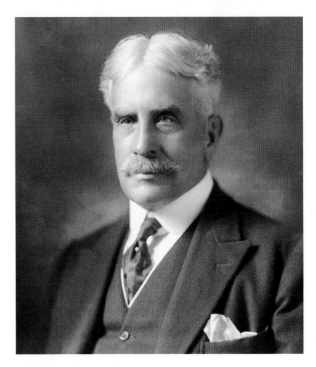

Sir Robert Laird Borden was prime minister of Canada when the federal government created the Canadian National Railway Company.

CN played a key role in nation building in the early 1920s, moving goods and people from coast to coast.

Launching the Railway

F ollowing the establishment of the crown corporation, the government put a board of management in charge of the Canadian National Railway Company. The board in turn hired a railway **executive** from the United States to be the company's president. Henry Worth Thornton had a distinguished career in railways. He had been the superintendent of the Long Island Rail Road prior to World War I and had been the general manager of England's Great

Henry Worth Thornton was appointed president of the Canadian National Railway Company in 1922.

Eastern Railway from 1914 to 1922. As president of Canadian National, it was his job to turn these struggling rail companies into a success story.

Prairie Potential
Thornton focussed his attention on expanding the network already in place. His goal was to continue the westward

Canadian National

Milestones

FIRST 4-8-4 LOCOMOTIVE
CN acquired its first a 4-8-4 Confederation locomotive in 1927.

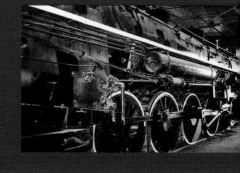

expansion, laying track in areas that had no rail service. In doing this, he hoped to encourage more settlement in these areas and develop a clientele of both passengers and trade.

Sensing the potential of the Prairies, Thornton directed the company to begin developing facilities that would encourage people to come to the area to farm. In Saskatchewan alone, the company set up more than 1,500 grain elevators, 500 train stations, and 400 stock yards. This provided farmers with access to transportation so they could get their wheat and cattle to market. As a result of this strategy, towns formed along the rail lines, and the railway began to turn a **profit**.

Travel in Comfort

This surplus cash allowed the company to **invest** in improvements that would grow its customer base. One such development was the construction of several luxury resort hotels designed to promote

rail travel. Grand hotels, such as the Saskatoon's Bessborough, Montreal's Queen Elizabeth Hotel, and the Hotel Nova Scotian in Halifax, assured customers that a comfortable stay awaited them at their destination. During this time, CN also acquired several steamships to move passengers and import and export goods.

The Bessborough Hotel opened in 1935. The hotel remains in operation to this day and is considered one of Saskatoon's best-known landmarks.

FIRST RADIO NETWORK

CN created the Canadian National Railways Radio Department in 1923 to provide entertainment for its passengers. This was Canada's first radio network.

FIRST DIESEL ELECTRIC PASSENGER LOCOMOTIVE

CN Rail placed its first diesel electric passenger locomotive into service on August 26, 1929.

Changing Times

The growth and expansion Canadian National experienced throughout the 1920s came to an abrupt halt in 1929, with the onset of the **Great Depression**. With the economy struggling worldwide, all industries, including the railways, felt the effects. CN's passenger service slowed significantly. People did not have the money to travel anywhere, and when they did, they were more likely to travel by car or bus. For the next 10 years, CN struggled to keep its passenger trains moving. The company had to close stations and cut staff hours in order to survive this trying time.

Taking to the Air

Canadian National also knew that it had to come up with new ways to do business. In 1937, it worked with the federal government to form its own air service. Called Trans-Canada Airlines, the **subsidiary** began flying Canadians across the country. When the government later cancelled a $1 billion debt that Canadian National owed, the company was able to gain a more stable financial foothold. It was soon taking steps to update its locomotive fleet.

The new locomotives proved to be a valuable asset to both the company and the country. In 1939, Canada entered World War II. The new locomotives helped transport troops to port for overseas service. This job alone helped keep the company afloat during tough economic times.

Rebirth and Renewal

Following the war years, Canadian National entered a new phase of development. The 1950s and 1960s saw a period of great growth and expansion for the company. These changes were spearheaded by then President and Chairman Donald Gordon. Gordon was appointed head of CN in 1950. It was a difficult time for CN, as the company was once again faced with declining passenger

Canadian National built the CN Tower as a TV and radio communication platform for the city of Toronto. It is the largest free-standing structure in the western hemisphere.

Trans-Canada Airlines changed its name to Air Canada in 1965. Twelve years later, it dissolved its partnership with Canadian National and became a stand-alone company.

business. Gordon was hired to find ways to invigorate what many considered a fading relic of transportation's past.

Gordon decided that, even though it would be expensive, the best course of action was to modernize the rail company. He supervised the conversion of CN's steam locomotives to diesel engines and had electronic signalling installed along CN tracks. To offset the costs involved, he took steps to streamline the company's operations by reducing the number of CN subsidiaries from 80 to 30.

A Move toward Profitability

By the end of the 1970s, CN had seen significant growth. Much of this growth came through its subsidiaries. Through CN Real Estate, the company owned and developed several properties in major Canadian cities, including the CN Tower. As well, its trucking company was moving goods across the country as CNX/CN Trucking. CN was also seeking to develop mineral rights it owned in the western provinces.

In 1978, the company decided to **recapitalize** and become a for-profit crown corporation. In the past, the company had relied on the government to assume its debt. As a for-profit corporation, it would focus on making a profit and using that profit to pay off its own debts and make its own **capital expenditures**. Recapitalizing helped CN reposition itself in the marketplace. It began to access financial markets to generate further capital for investment and expansion.

In 1977, CN formed Via Rail Canada Incorporated. Via Rail remained a CN subsidiary until 1978 when it became a crown corporation in its own right.

Making Room for Growth

CN continued to undergo significant changes throughout the 1980s and 1990s. As a for-profit company, CN had to focus on making money. Besides expanding into new markets, the company had to make cuts to areas that were draining its finances.

Forces of Change

Over the years, CN had **diversified** into areas that were unrelated to transportation. When the cuts came, the company began to **divest** itself of the properties and subsidiaries that did not relate directly to its business. One of the first subsidiaries to be sold was the CN's

Paul Tellier played a key role in expanding CN's network so that it extended south to the Gulf of Mexico. This was accomplished mainly through the purchase of U.S. rail lines.

telecommunications firm. It then sold its hotel chain to its main rival, Canadian Pacific. These sales helped the company reduce its debt load.

However, there was still more work to do. Trains no longer played the role in Canadian life that they once did. Roads had been built into remote areas that were once accessible only by train. Many CN rail lines had little traffic and were no longer profitable. The company began taking steps to sell these lines. Those that could not be sold were abandoned.

Even with these extreme measures, the debt remained. By the early 1990s, CN was reporting financial losses of more than $840 million. In 1992, Canadian Prime Minister Brian Mulroney stepped in and appointed Paul Tellier as CN's president and Chief Executive Officer. Tellier was to turn the company's finances around and prepare it for **privatization**.

To do this, Tellier continued selling off many of its **non-core assets**. The CN Tower was sold in 1992, and other real estate holdings soon followed. More rail lines were also sold or abandoned during this time. Almost 14,000 CN employees lost their jobs.

The privatization of CN gave the company the lift that it needed. The selling of shares alone brought in $2.2 billion. By 1996, CN had recorded profits of $850 million.

On July 1, 1999, CN purchased the U.S. rail company Illinois Central for $2.4 billion. The purchase included a track that stretched from Chicago, Illinois, to New Orleans, Louisiana. This additional track gave CN important access to ports in the Gulf of Mexico. It also made CN the fifth largest railway in North America.

Multi-billionaire and Microsoft co-founder Bill Gates is the largest shareholder of CN stocks, owning almost 12 percent of the company.

A Private Success

After years of challenge as a crown corporation, the company was finally in a position to become a private company. On July 13, 1995, the CN **Commercialization** Act was enacted into law, and the federal government sold its shares in CN to private investors. However, the government left two provisions in the act that ensured the company would remain Canadian. First, no individual or corporation could own more than 15 percent of the company. Second, the company's headquarters had to stay in Montreal, Quebec. Both of these rules were important because many of the people who bought the government's shares were Americans.

CN Rail Lines

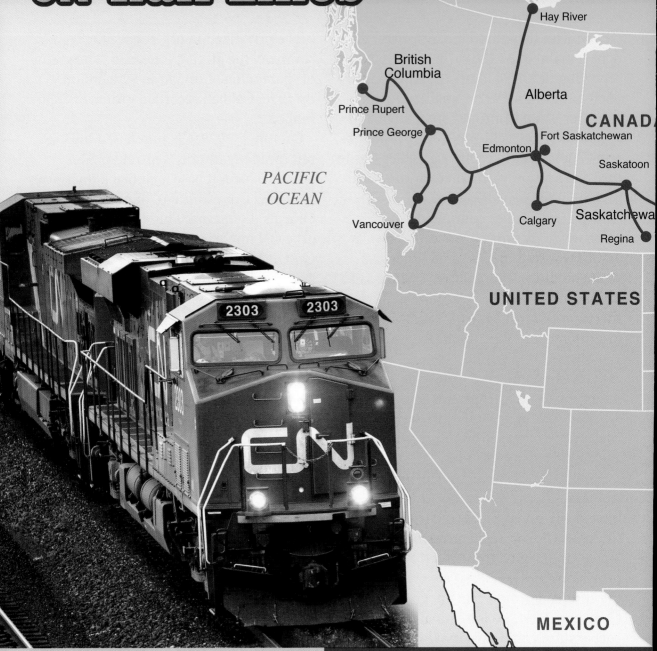

British Columbia

Hay River

Alberta

Prince Rupert

Prince George

Edmonton

Fort Saskatchewan

CANADA

Saskatoon

PACIFIC
OCEAN

Calgary

Saskatchewa

Vancouver

Regina

UNITED STATES

MEXICO

C N's rail network extends from one end of the country to the other, and into the United States. Its trains roll into three major ports in North America. This allows CN to ship freight to or from anywhere in the world.

Port of Vancouver

Vancouver is the home of Canada's busiest seaport. The port provides shipping services to and from Asia, including China and Japan.

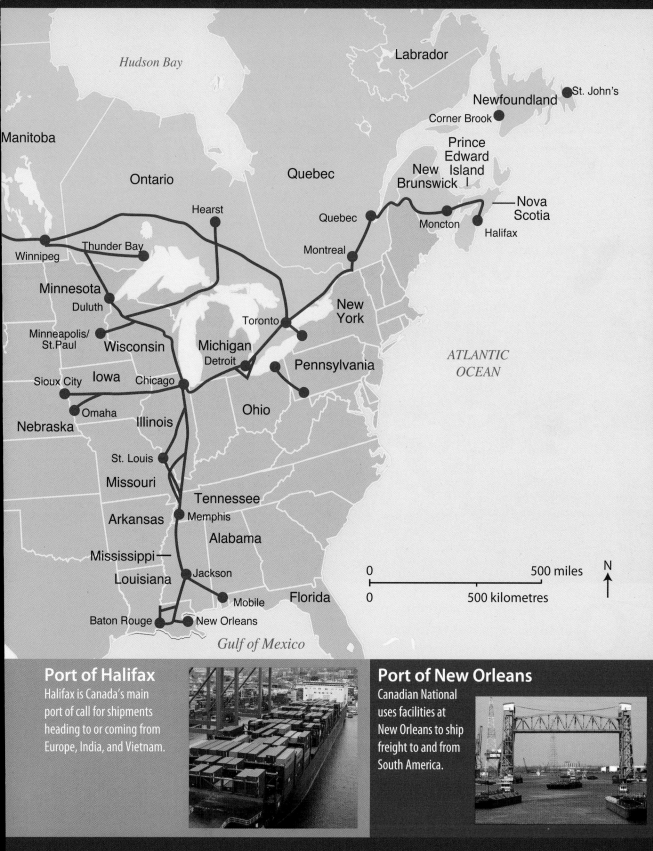

Hudson Bay

Labrador

Newfoundland

St. John's

Corner Brook

Manitoba

Ontario

Quebec

Prince
Edward
Island

New
Brunswick

Nova
Scotia

Hearst

Quebec

Moncton

Halifax

Montreal

Winnipeg

Thunder Bay

Minnesota

Duluth

New
York

Minneapolis/
St.Paul

Wisconsin

Toronto

ATLANTIC
OCEAN

Sioux City

Iowa

Michigan

Detroit

Chicago

Pennsylvania

Omaha

Ohio

Nebraska

Illinois

St. Louis

Missouri

Tennessee

Arkansas

Memphis

Alabama

Mississippi

Jackson

Louisiana

Florida

Baton Rouge

Mobile

New Orleans

Gulf of Mexico

0   500 miles

0   500 kilometres

N

Port of Halifax
Halifax is Canada's main port of call for shipments heading to or coming from Europe, India, and Vietnam.

Port of New Orleans
Canadian National uses facilities at New Orleans to ship freight to and from South America.

The Canadian National Brand

One of the most important aspects of any company is its brand. Many experts say that a company's brand is its promise to its customers. A company's brand should tell a customer what is important to that company, what the customer can expect from the company, and what the company values. Some companies spend months, and even years, developing a strong brand. A brand can include a **logo** and a **slogan**.

CN built new rail lines throughout the 1950s to access new markets. The company logo was front and centre at the last spike ceremonies for these lines.

These elements of branding help to provide a unique corporate identity and attract customers.

CN prides itself in being a company that strives for quality in everything it does. It wants the public to view it as an open, efficient, and forward-thinking organization. All of its branding has been created around these traits.

A Progressive Brand

The CN logo is one of the most-recognized corporate symbols in Canada. The logo was created in 1960. It was part of a plan to rebrand the company as a progressive and modern organization. This re-branding was to counter the reputation railways had of being old and outdated.

The logo is a simple design, featuring the letters *C* and *N* flowing one into the other as if in motion. The continuous line of text is meant to represent the movement of people and products from one point to another. The logo is also meant to represent the bilingual nature of Canada. In English, CN represents Canadian National. In French, it stands for Canadien National.

The People's Railway

CN has used several slogans over the years. Each has represented the company at a certain point in its history. One of the first slogans it used was "Serves All Canada." Placed on boxcars, it told customers that CN was a national company that served the nation's needs. Later, CN adopted the slogan, "The people's railway." This branding was based on the idea that Canadians, and their industries, were on the move. The slogan positioned CN as a partner to the people in their desire to build a life for themselves and expand their own businesses.

Today, CN's slogan is "North America's Railroad." These words let people know that the company's services extend beyond the Canadian border.

What's in a Name?

Canadian National's brand has gone through many changes as the demand for rail transportation has changed in Canada. However, one constant for the company has been its name.

Even though the company refers to itself as CN, the letters are known to represent Canadian National. When first created, the full name of the company was Canadian National Railway Company. This represented the company's status as a crown corporation and as a company that served the nation.

As the Canadian National Railway Company extended its reach beyond rail transportation, the company opted to stop using the word "Railway" in its marketing. It was at about this time that the company rebranded itself as CN and adopted its current logo.

In 1993, CN decided to add North America to its name as a way of showing the reach of its operations. The use of CN North America only lasted for about a year before the company returned to using the name CN. This name, however, is still only a form of branding. The company's legal name remains Canadian National Railway Company.

The Art of Selling

CN uses a variety of marketing strategies to promote and sell its services. Some strategies are designed to promote the company itself. Others are designed to attract a specific type of customer. Marketing strategies such as advertising and **sponsorships** help to keep CN's name active in the marketplace.

Advertising

CN is constantly looking for ways to improve its services and sell to more markets. Its marketing team develops major ad **campaigns** for the company. Many of these ads are placed strategically so that they appear

The CN International Grand Prix is held every September at Spruce Meadows. Its purse is worth $1 million to the winner.

in publications specifically related to shipping, warehousing, and **supply chain management**.

The company also produces numerous brochures and pamphlets that can be distributed upon request and when the sales team attends trade shows. The company's trade show booths themselves are a form of advertising. Often featuring large posters and banners, they promote the company's services and commitment to meeting their customers' needs.

Sponsorships

Advertising is not always intended to make a direct sale. Some advertising is created to ensure that the company's name remains in the public eye. CN participates in a number of commercial sponsorship programs that put its name at the forefront of various events and institutions. The British Columbia city of Prince George, for instance, is home to the CN Centre. This 5,967-seat arena hosts numerous concerts and hockey games throughout the year. CN bought the **naming rights** to the arena in 2005 to promote the company within the community and the country.

CN also lends its name to several sporting events. It serves as the **title sponsor** for the annual CN International Grand Prix horse-jumping event at Calgary's Spruce Meadows Masters Tournament, as well as the CN Future Links program, which nurtures up-and-coming youth golfers.

The Brand on Sale

Another form of advertising CN uses is brand-specific merchandise. CN is aware that there are fans of railways and railway travel. These people like to collect merchandise that features logos of railway lines. As a result, CN has developed a line of products that feature the company logo. Some of these products include baseball caps, coffee mugs, t-shirts, watches, and belt buckles.

People who buy this merchandise can sometimes be seen in public wearing and using it. In this way, the CN logo is visible in non-traditional markets and may attract new customers. The public use of the merchandise also keeps the CN brand relevant in the minds of people all across North America, and internationally as well.

CN served as title sponsor for the Canadian Women's Open from 2006 to 2013.

At Your Service

Today, the Canadian National Railway Company is a leader in freight delivery. The company prides itself on delivering excellent customer service, with on-time deliveries and careful handling of products. Over the decades, CN has developed many innovative and valuable services to support its customers.

Rail Service

CN's rail tracks cover more than 30,000 kilometres of North America. This range gives freight customers access to 75 percent of the North American market and a significant portion of the international market. The company is equipped to provide shipping for consumer products as well as hazardous materials. It ships goods in boxcars, hoppers, tankers, and intermodal containers loaded onto flat cars.

Road Service

With approximately 700 drivers and a fleet of 6,000 trucks, CNTL, CN's trucking service, is capable of delivering 1,300 loads a day. CNTL is closely associated with the CN's intermodal service. Its trucks deliver goods within a 800-kilometre radius of CN's 19 intermodal train terminals.

Intermodal Service

CN's intermodal service allows products to be shipped over long distances with minimal fuss. The intermodal container is placed on a train for the long-haul land journey. From there, it can be either loaded onto a ship for international service or hooked up to a truck for local door-to-door service. CN's containers are temperature-controlled, allowing for the shipping of a variety of products.

Warehousing and Distribution

Understanding that some customers need storage space for their products, CN operates more than 80 warehouse facilities throughout North America. These facilities account for more than 120,000 square metres of storage space. The warehouses and **distribution centres** have been built to handle specific products, including forest products, grains and other crops, bulk products, metals, and automotive products. Most of the facilities are able to warehouse more than one type of product.

Conducting the Business

A company the size of CN requires the skills of many people. The corporate team is responsible for planning the company's future path. They decide on capital expenditures, route expansion and closure, and how to keep company costs under control.

President

The president of a company is responsible for the operation of all of the company's departments. Corporate presidents ensure that all divisions are running smoothly and are keeping within budget. The president is also responsible for the company's long-term planning. Working alongside other executives and senior management, he or she determines the direction the company will take over the next few years. The president then ensures that the appropriate steps are taken to realize this plan while keeping costs under control.

CN President: Claude Mongeau
Education: Masters of Business
  Administration (MBA), McGill University
Joined CN: 1994

Chairperson

The chairperson is the leader of a company's board of directors. A board of directors is a group of people elected or appointed to oversee the activities of a company. Board members meet and discuss important issues dealing with the company. They establish company policies and objectives, select the chief executive, approve annual budgets, and set the salaries of company management. As the leader of the board, the chairperson directs meetings and makes sure board members understand the issues under review.

CN Chairman: David McLean
Education: Bachelor of Arts and Bachelor of
  Law, University of Alberta, 1962
Joined CN: 1979

Chief Financial Officer

The chief financial officer (CFO) of a company is responsible for the company's financial organization, including accounting, financial reporting, taxation, financial planning and analysis, **internal audit**, pension administration, investor relations, and the procurement of corporate real estate. The CFO monitors the company's financial performance and assesses the financial viability of the company's long-term plans. He or she plays a key role in a company's decision-making process.

CN Chief Financial Officer: Luc Jobin
Education: Chartered Accountant Accreditation, Canadian Institute of Chartered Accountants
Joined CN: 2009

Chief Information Officer

A company's chief information officer (CIO) oversees all aspects relating to information technology and computer systems and logistics. These include computer networks within the company, mobile technologies such as smart phones and devices, voice and data communications, and web technology. The CIO works with a team of engineers and managers to maintain effective communication with staff and customers. A CIO works closely with the president to find effective solutions to fast and accurate customer service, delivery of services, and movement of products such as freight.

CN Chief Information Officer: James Bright
Education: MBA, Concordia University
Joined CN: 1974

Working the Rails

I n 2012, more than 23,000 people powered CN in both Canada and the United States. These people have a wide range of skills and specializations. Some people work in administrative positions. Others work in marketing and sales. Still, it is the people responsible for operating the rails that remain the core of the company. Making sure the trains get to their destinations safely and on time is key to the company's success.

Locomotive Engineers

One of the most visible jobs at CN is that of the locomotive engineer. These engineers are the people who operate the trains. To maneuver the train from one point to the next, locomotive engineers

A locomotive engineer often gains experience in other positions, starting as either a brakeman or a conductor, before taking control of the locomotive.

must know the physical characteristics of a railroad and be able to anticipate the handling of inclines, declines, turns, and tunnels. They must also know where the stations are and be aware of rules and regulations, including speed limits. Locomotive engineers need to have excellent concentration and time management skills. Most locomotive engineers have received certification qualifying them to operate the train.

Rail Traffic Controller

Train movement is the heart of CN

Sales and marketing agents work as a team to develop marketing campaigns and strategies.

operations. A rail traffic controller is responsible for directing and managing the movement of trains. At CN, there are dozens of rail traffic controllers (RTCs) supervising hundreds of trains over thousands of kilometres of track. Their job is to plan and schedule the safe movement of all rail vehicles, including maintenance equipment. RTCs must have a strong working knowledge of train operation and rail travel. They must know about all rail equipment as well as train signals. Much of their skill is learned on the job as part of a team of crew dispatchers.

Sales and Marketing Agents

Sales and marketing agents are responsible for selling a product or service to new and existing customers. It is their job to build and maintain relationships with the people and companies that use CN's services. To do this, they need to know the products and services the company offers. A job in sales and marketing usually requires a degree in business or economics. Agents must have a solid understanding of selling techniques, product promotion, and advertising. Sales agents have to possess excellent people skills and work well with others.

Rail traffic controllers work at a desktop workstation, where they monitor train activity on computer screens. They communicate with train personnel by radio.

Canadian National FAQs

CN operates on a variety of levels, from corporate to front line. Anyone wanting to become a member of the team should learn more about the company and its operations.

DOES CN STILL OPERATE ITS PASSENGER SERVICE?

Although VIA Rail took over CN's passenger service in 1978, CN still has a few passenger trains running on its lines, including a small commuter operation between Sault Ste. Marie and Hearst, Ontario, as well as a railbus service between Seton Portage and Lillooet in British Columbia.

CAN CN SHIP ANYWHERE IN NORTH AMERICA?

CN serves all major Canadian markets and 14 states in the United States. Through its intermodal service, CN can reach 75 percent of the U.S. population by either train or truck.

IS CN STILL A CROWN CORPORATION?

CN was owned and run by the Canadian government from 1919 to 1995. In 1995, the federal government offered the company for sale to **shareholders**, making it a publicly traded company.

WHERE IS CN'S HEAD OFFICE?

CN's headquarters are located in the downtown core of Montreal, Quebec. The company also has regional offices and operations centres in various locations throughout North America.

WHERE ARE CN'S LOCOMOTIVES BUILT?

In the past, most of CN's locomotives were built in Montreal, Quebec, and New York City. The company's most recent purchases have been manufactured in the United States.

HOW CAN I GET A JOB WITH CN?

People interested in working for CN can apply directly to the company through its website. CN's website provides information on the various divisions and positions within the company as well as a list of job openings. The list includes the job description, the qualifications required, and the location of the job.

All Aboard

Like any business, CN understands that customers are key to the company's success. It is committed to keeping its regular customers and attracting others. CN makes sure that it has systems in place to quickly address its customers' questions and concerns. CN believes in building relationships with its customers. It accomplishes this in several ways.

Customer Support

CN has a team of customer service representatives available to discuss any issues or concerns a customer may have. To allow easy access to this assistance, reps can be reached via phone or over the internet. As well, the company's website

CN understands the importance of timely shipping. The online tracking system allows customers to know where their shipment is at all points along the line.

offers areas for the customer to locate shipping rates, arrange pickups, and track their shipments.

Staying Informed

Communication is a key component to building relationships. CN works hard to keep its customers informed about the direction the company is taking and any changes it is undergoing. The CN website has a section devoted to customer care. Here, customers will find press releases regarding the recent developments, such as new products and services, as well as the company's position on the different issues facing it. The site also features events that may be of interest to CN's customers. These events can include conferences, trade shows, and meetings. CN is also active in social media, communicating news through Facebook, Twitter, and LinkedIn. These sites help CN stay in touch with its customers and encourage a dialogue with them.

Keeping in Touch

Customer feedback plays an important role in the decisions CN makes regarding its operations. The company website has an area for customers to register concerns and make comments about the products and services CN offers. CN reviews these comments regularly and makes every effort to solve problems. Sometimes, the issues involve one shipment and are easily resolved. Other issues, however, can result in major corporate changes. In 2012, for instance, customers on the Prairies experienced significant delays of shipments due to poor weather conditions. Several customers complained about the impact the delays had on their businesses. CN's response was immediate. The company's president contacted each customer personally and committed to improving its service. In 2013, CN announced that it was upgrading its rail lines across the Prairies at a cost of about $100 million.

Most of CN's Prairie upgrade will take place on the main line between Edmonton, Alberta, and Winnipeg, Manitoba.

Giving Back

Being a responsible **corporate citizen** is an important part of the CN's business model. The company believes in giving back to the community through education and safety initiatives. It also believes strongly in **sustainability**. The company has been in existence for almost 100 years and has no plans to stop operations. Its leaders know that decisions they make today will affect generations to come.

Going Green

CN has long been committed to the concept of environmental stewardship. This means caring for the environment and reducing the

For shipments travelling more than 1,600 kilometres, using intermodal transport cuts fuel use and greenhouse gas emissions by 65 percent relative to truck transport alone.

company's **environmental footprint**. Rail transportation is already an environmentally friendly way to ship goods. However, CN realizes that there can be room for improvement. CN has signed on to the U.S. SmartWay Agreement, a program that seeks to eliminate 33 to 60 million tonnes of carbon dioxide emissions from the transportation industry. This initiative could save 150 million barrels of oil per year. That equates to taking 12 million cars off the road.

CN Stronger Communities Fund

CN supports several not-for-profit organizations through its CN Stronger Communities Fund. Its contributions have been in the form of responsible community investments. The company focusses its efforts on health and safety for young people and on transportation education. Between 2006 and 2012, CN raised more than $8.2 million for children's hospitals across Canada. It also supports organizations that promote healthy lifestyles for kids.

As well, CN supports charities such as the United Way and Centraide. These agencies are in line with CN's commitment to improve lives and build communities. The company and its employees have contributed more than $1 million to these charities annually.

CN Railroaders in the Community

Many CN employees and retirees donate their time to various community-based charitable organizations. Volunteering at homeless shelters and coaching amateur sports groups are just two ways that these people contribute to their communities. To reward these dedicated employees, CN developed the CN Railroaders in the Community program. This program offers cash grants to charitable organizations that have CN employees among their volunteers. Besides helping the organizations directly, these grants encourage CN employees to stay active in the community.

CN's safety programs teach children to be careful around rail crossings and tracks.

CN offers its employees a matched-fundraising program. When an employee participates in a fundraising event, such as a marathon, the company will match the money he or she raises.

Competitors

When CN was formed, it amalgamated a group of railways under one name. This action reduced the number of competitors on Canada's railways. Eventually, there were only two main competitors in Canada's rail transportation industry—Canadian National and Canadian Pacific.

As CN diversified into other businesses and other markets, it began to acquire other competitors. Today, the company competes with railways in the United States as well as Canada. It also competes with trucking companies. The goals of these companies are very similar. All of them want to be their customers' first choice when they need to ship goods from one point to another.

Canadian Pacific Railway

Founded in 1881, Canadian Pacific Railway was Canada's first transcontinental railway, connecting British Columbia with eastern Canada. By the time CN was formed, CPR had established itself in the industry of tourism. Its passenger trains were considered the height of luxury, with their own sleeping and dining cars, and as CN would later do as well, CPR had built its own first-class hotels, including Alberta's Chateau Lake Louise, along its route. Today, CPR operates 22,500 kilometres of track in both Canada and the United States. It is second only to CN in rail business in Canada. However, in the United States, its presence is small compared to CN.

TransForce Inc.

With at least 6,700 vehicles and 12,000 trailers, TransForce Inc. is one of Canada's leading transportation companies. It specializes in road transportation services.

TransForce provides transportation services for a variety of industries, including retail, energy, automotives, mining, and forestry. Besides being a trucking company, it also operates several courier companies, including Loomis Express, Dynamex, and Canpar Courier. Two-thirds of the company's business is in Eastern Canada. However, the company has recently started operating in the United States. TransForce began in 1957 as a local trucking firm in Quebec. It has grown itself mainly through the acquisition of other companies. In 2011, its revenues exceeded $2.7 billion.

Union Pacific Railroad

Union Pacific Railroad is the largest rail network in the United States. It operates more than 8,000 locomotives on 51,500 kilometres of track in 23 states, mainly in the western part of the country. Its rail connections also allow it to transfer shipments into Mexico and Canada. At the end of 2012, Union Pacific employed more than 45,000 employees and posted revenues of $19.7 billion.

The company was **incorporated** in 1862 in an act approved by U. S. President Abraham Lincoln. The Pacific Railroad Act of 1862 started construction of railroads from the Missouri River to the Pacific Ocean. It was hoped that such a railroad would keep the United States together as a country.

Today, the company has one of the busiest rail networks in the United States. Much of its business involves transporting large shipments from west coast ports to inland locations. These shipments can include products ranging from agricultural and automotive goods to chemicals and coal. Like CN, Union Pacific also offers intermodal service.

Charting Success

OPERATING REVENUES

Annual Revenues ($ in Millions)

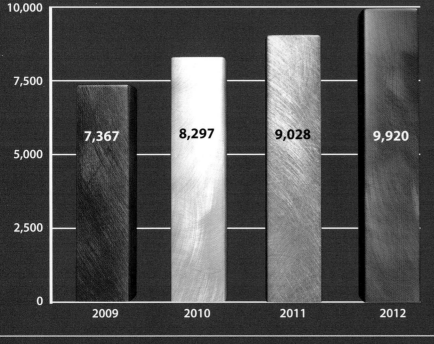

Year	Revenue
2009	7,367
2010	8,297
2011	9,028
2012	9,920

CN's revenues have been on a steady climb in recent years, indicating that companies are seeing the benefits of rail shipping.

Annual Carloads

Rail is becoming a popular way to move goods across North America. In recent years, CN has seen steady growth in the number of carloads its trains are carrying.

= 1,000,000 carloads

2009

2010

2011

2012

Revenue Distribution

Of the $9.9 billion CN earned in revenue in 2012, most of it came from overseas traffic.

Overseas Traffic 32%

US Domestic Traffic 17%

Transborder Traffic 29%

Canadian Domestic Traffic 22%

Environmental Impact

The environmental impact of its shipping methods is important to CN. This chart compares the greenhouse gas emissions for a shipment containing 20,000 tonnes of consumer goods from the port at Prince Rupert, British Columbia, to CN's Brampton, Ontario intermodal terminal, using both rail and truck. Shipping by rail creates fewer carbon dioxide (CO_2) emissions.

Port of Prince Rupert, BC, to Brampton, ON Intermodal Terminal

Truck Transport

Distance 4, 795 km	CO2 emissions (tonnes) 4,859

Rail Transport

Distance 4, 795 km	CO2 emissions (tonnes) 1,712

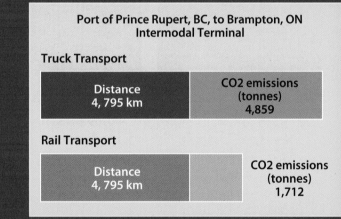

Innovation and Technology

The Canadian National Railway Company was born out of technology and **industrialization**. Over the decades, CN has had to be creative and innovative in its delivery of shipping services to its customers. Since its creation, CN has been an industry leader in research and development of railway

ENVIRONMENT

Fuel Emissions

In its effort to control its greenhouse gas emissions, CN began experimenting with engines that run on a mix of liquefied natural gas and diesel fuel. Natural gas makes up the bulk of the fuel, at 90 percent. It is expected that these engines will reduce CN's carbon dioxide output by about 30 percent. Its nitrogen oxide emissions will be reduced by 70 percent. Testing on the engines began in 2013 in northern Alberta.

TECHNOLOGY

SmartYard

CN uses a vast network of computer systems and programs to manage its large operation. One program it has developed to keep track of its trains is called SmartYard. This software application collects real-time data from specific points on the tracks. It uses this information to determine the flow of traffic in and out of the railyards. The program allows **yardmasters** to manage and schedule the movement of dozens of trains at a time.

CUSTOMER SERVICE

Shipment Tracking

Knowing where a shipment is and when to expect its arrival is an important part of CN's customer service. Besides having customer service representatives, CN developed a program called Automate that allows customers to track their shipments. The system is able to track up to 240 separate shipments. Once the shipment is delivered, the customer can use another system, called Automated Railcar Release, to release the railcars back to CN.

safety systems and logistics management. Today, it continues to develop newer, more fuel efficient equipment.

CN's commitment to customer service has also resulted in several developments. The company wants its customers to be able to track their shipments to their destinations. It is always monitoring its existing systems to see if there are areas that can be improved.

SAFETY

Network and Security

CN moves highly sensitive and sometimes dangerous goods through its system. The company uses a number of new technologies to protect the company and the public from harm. More than 9,500 kilometres of fibre optic cables run along CN's rail lines. The cables record and send data to CN's communications centres. The company also uses wireless, satellite, and 3-D imaging technology to monitor and anticipate security and safety issues.

SAFETY

Track Geometry Vehicle

CN uses a high-tech track geometry vehicle to monitor and report on track conditions. This self-propelled track vehicle electronically inspects track curvature, alignment, and levels of all rail lines in CN's network. The system uses high-speed cameras and optical recognition equipment to detect flaws in the lines. Data collected from the vehicle allows CN to make repairs to the tracks where needed.

OPERATIONS

Locomotive Simulators

CN uses eight state-of-the-art portable locomotive simulators to train engineers and rail transport managers. The simulators recreate exact train handling and track conditions, and prepare drivers for different situations that can occur on the route. Information gathered during simulation helps CN adjust its operations, improving efficiency of deliveries.

CN is now one of the most successful railway companies in North America. However, in its early days, it would have been difficult to imagine it achieving its current status. As a crown corporation, the company was constantly in debt, relying on help from the government to survive. It was only after the company went public that it was able to find its financial footing. Still, even though it is now a stable company, CN continues to face challenges that threaten the security and reputation it has achieved.

Early Challenges

Even though CN was formed from the merging of several struggling rail companies, it was able to start turning profits by the mid-1920s. Then, the Great Depression hit in 1929. The world economy was affected severely. At CN, both business and leisure traffic fell, leading to cuts in wages and staff layoffs. By 1932, CN's revenues had fallen 40 percent from their peak in 1928. The rise of the automobile brought further challenges, and people could travel by bus on newly built all-weather highways. They could also ship goods by truck at a much lower cost than by rail.

Over the next few years, CN took steps to keep the company stable and attract more passengers. It purchased dome cars so people could view the scenery as they travelled across the country. It also continued to diversify, extending its portfolio into real estate and other transportation services. However, these actions were not successful in relieving the company's debt load. As a result, CN was constantly having to **restructure** itself, selling off ventures that were not making money and streamlining its staff and systems.

Tragedy on the Rails

On September 1, 1947, a CN passenger train was carrying vacationers toward Dugald, Manitoba, when it collided head on with a standing train. The result was devastating. The older CN coaches were made of wood and lit by gas-burning lights. Flames spread at a terrifying rate. Thirty-one people lost their lives.

An inquest after the tragedy concluded that most of the people had died as a result of the wooden coaches catching fire. In the years following the accident, CN re-equipped the passenger trains travelling all of its major routes with lightweight steel passenger cars.

Labour Woes

CN has employed thousands of people over the decades. Managing such a large work force comes with many challenges. Tensions between management and rail workers came to a head in 1950 when 130,000 workers went on **strike** over their hours of work. The strike brought rail transport to a standstill from coast to coast. At the time, rail transport was considered an essential service. To get the trains on the tracks again, the federal government implemented back-to-work legislation for the first time. Within days, the government forced the strikers back to work.

In 2004, approximately 5,000 CN workers went on strike over wages, work hours, and benefits.

This has not stopped CN workers from walking off the job. In 2009, CN's locomotive engineers went on strike over a proposed increase to their monthly mileage cap. The engineers were concerned that being required to travel more kilometres each month would create safety issues. The strike ended when CN agreed to maintain the current mileage cap.

The Future

In 2013, CN opened a intermodal terminal on the outskirts of Calgary, Alberta. The decision to build there was due to the rapid growth in the city and surrounding area.

CN sees many opportunities for growth as it continues to explore new ways to serve its customers. The company serves a number of other industries. As these industries grow, their shipping and storage needs will change. CN has several initiatives to handle this growth and offer new products and services to its customers. At the same time, the company realizes that it must constantly pursue new customers and new markets, and be prepared to meet their needs as well.

Investment in the Future

In 2013, CN announced that it would be spending approximately $1.9 billion to upgrade its railway networks in North America. The company will spend more than $1 billion on improving its track **infrastructure** alone. This will begin with an inspection of all its lines. It will then repair or replace rails and ties, as well as fix any bridges in need of work. It will also seek to improve the productivity of its rail network by adopting new technology and improving its work flow.

CN plans to spend about $700 million on improving its distribution centres. Improvements to these operations will make the transfer of freight from train to truck even more efficient. Some of this money will finance the construction of a new intermodal terminal in Illinois. More than $200 million will be spent to acquire new locomotives and vehicles for trucking.

New Markets

In recent years, CN has begun promoting itself internationally. In 2012, the company opened a sales office in India to complement representation already in Vietnam, China, and other parts of Asia. CN sees Asia as an emerging market that will soon be shipping products to and from Canada. The company is specifically monitoring the shipping of bitumen from the Alberta oil sands. China is a heavy oil user, and Alberta oil sands companies are anxious to ship there. However, a proposed oil pipeline through British Columbia has been stalled by government discussions. CN sees the opportunity to promote the shipping of bitumen by rail to ports in Alaska. The bitumen could then be loaded onto tankers and shipped to the Asian market. Rail lines have been used to ship oil and oil products for years. They face fewer restrictions than pipelines. By shipping to Alaska instead of British Columbia, the oil sands companies could circumvent the issue of pipeline construction.

Pipelines are scrutinized for their environmental impact. Their construction often affects fragile ecosystems. Once built, they can be at risk of leaks and breaks.

Timeline

1919 On June 6, the Canadian National Railway Company is incorporated as a crown corporation, owned and operated by the Canadian federal government.

1922

Sir Henry Worth Thornton is appointed as CN's first president.

1923 CN begins making radio broadcasts. These broadcasts are aired throughout their passenger cars.

1927 CN acquires its first 4-8-4 Confederation locomotive.

1929 CN's first diesel-electric locomotive is put into operation.

1937 Trans-Canada Airlines, later known as Air Canada, begins operating as a subsidiary of CN Rail.

1947 A CN train collides head-on with another train near Dugald, Manitoba. Thirty-one people lose their lives.

1976

CN completes construction of the CN Tower, the world's largest free-standing structure at the time.

1978 CN recapitalizes, becoming a for-profit crown corporation.

1978 VIA Rail assumes the management of CN's passenger rail service.

1995 On November 17, the Canadian government decides to privatize CN. The federal government profits $2.2 billion from the sale.

1999 The purchase of the Illinois Central Corporation signals CN's entrance into the U.S. market. The purchase gives CN access to the New Orleans port in the Gulf of Mexico.

2001 CN acquires U.S. railway Wisconsin Central for $1.2 billion.

2003 CN acquires Canada's third-largest rail company, BC Rail Ltd., for $1 billion.

2013 CN begins testing locomotives fuelled primarily by natural gas, improving fuel efficiency and environmental responsibility.

2013 CN announces it is upgrading its rail lines across Canada's Prairie Provinces.

Canadian National Railway Top 10

A CN locomotive can weigh more than 200 tonnes.

Retail giant Wal-Mart Canada awarded CN its Innovator of the Year Award in 2010 for the development of its "EcoTherm" temperature-controlled container, which keeps goods refrigerated without using heat.

The CN logo has been chosen as one of the Top 50 Corporate Logos of All Times by an international panel of designers.

Canadian National Railway Engine 6400 pulled the famous Royal Train when King George VI and his wife Queen Elizabeth visited Canada in 1939. Twelve cars, from CN and CP, were painted royal blue with gold and aluminum trim.

CN BEGAN OPERATING SCHOOL CARS IN NORTHERN ONTARIO BEGINNING IN 1926. THESE PORTABLE SCHOOLS OFFERED EDUCATION TO REMOTE CANADIAN COMMUNITIES THAT DID NOT HAVE SCHOOLS.

CANADIAN NATIONAL RAILWAYS

In 1968, CN introduced a new high-speed passenger train, the United Aircraft TurboTrain. It used gas turbines instead of diesel engines and was capable of reaching speeds of 160 kilometres per hour.

The longest wood trestle bridge in North America is CN's Rochfort Trestle bridge near Mayerthorpe, Alberta. Built in 1914, it is 736 metres long and 33.5 metres high.

A CN train can be more than 4 kilometres long and weigh almost 18,000 tonnes.

CNR Radio broadcast the first live hockey game in Canada on November 12, 1931. Known then as the General Motors Hockey Broadcast, it would later become Hockey Night in Canada. In the game, the Chicago Blackhawks defeated the Toronto Maple Leafs 2-1.

In 1995, the American Society of Civil Engineers declared the CN Tower one of the Seven Wonders of the Modern World.

Activity

A large part of CN's success has been maintaining excellent customer service. CN is committed to its customers and is constantly looking for ways to improve its customer service. One tool that companies use to determine customer satisfaction is a survey. Using CN as a business model, design your own customer service survey.

1 Research the customer groups that use CN's shipping service. Industries include retail, energy, forestry, metals, coal, and automobiles. Select a group to design a survey for.

2 Research the various shipping services CN offers. They include rail transport, trucking, and intermodal services. Does your customer group ship internationally or domestically?

4 Approach a local business in your area that might use shipping service. Ask if they would fill out your survey and give you feedback on your project.

3 Formulate questions you think would be important for CN to know. How often do they use shipping services? When are their peak seasons for shipping? Do they ship all over North America or just in certain regions?

Test Your Knowledge

1 When was CN incorporated as a crown corporation?

2 How many kilometres of track does CN operate?

3 What is the name of the CN shipping service that involves exchange of containers from train to truck?

4 Who was the first president of the Canadian National Railway Company?

5 When did VIA Rail take charge of CN's struggling passenger service?

6 The Canadian government privatized CN Rail by passing the CN Commercialization Act. What date was the Act passed?

7 Which three key ports do CN's trains access?

8 What is CN's current company slogan?

9 What is the name of CN's trucking company?

10 Which railway is CN's major competitor in Canada?

Glossary

campaigns: organized programs of advertisements

capital expenditures: purchases a company makes with its profits

commercialization: the process of turning an organization into a for-profit business

corporate citizen: a company that acts responsibly toward society

crown corporation: a company owned and operated by the government

distribution centres: warehouses that are stocked with products to be shipped to retailers, wholesalers, or consumers

diversified: varied products, operations, etc. in order to spread risk or to expand

divest: to free or get rid of

environmental footprint: a measure of the human impact on Earth's ecosystems

executive: a person with managerial authority in an organization

Great Depression: a period of economic crisis that began in 1929 and lasted through to 1939

incorporated: when a company becomes a legal corporation

industrialization: a time in a country's history when manufacturing and the use of heavy machinery begin to rise

infrastructure: the framework of a structure or system

intermodal: a shipping system that involves containers being loaded onto trains, and then transferred to trucks or ships

internal audit: the inspection of the accounting records and practices of a business

invest: to commit money in order to gain a financial return

logo: an easily recognizable image that represents a company

naming rights: the right to name an event or facility for a certain amount of time

non-core assets: things a company owns that are not very important to operations, such as buildings or land

privatization: the transfer of ownership from government to private companies

profit: the monetary return received on a business undertaking after all operating expenses have been met

public: a company that sells shares on the stock market

recapitalize: to restructure a company's finances so it can raise money and pay down money owed

restructure: reorganize a company for greater efficiency

revenues: income, or money coming in

shareholders: people who have bought shares in a company in the hopes of receive a percentage of money back as the company profits

slogan: a memorable quote that represents the company and sticks in the minds of its customers

sponsorships: supporting events or organizations by providing money or other resources in return for advertising space

strike: a stoppage of work as a form of protest for workers' rights

subsidiary: a company controlled by a larger company

supply chain management: operating and organizing the network of companies that provide products to end users

sustainability: the ability to continue for a long time

title sponsor: a form of sponsorship that allows a company to have its name as part of an event

transcontinental: across a continent, from sea to sea

yardmasters: the people in charge of a railroad yard

Index